1st Level Maths

1B

Practice Workbook 2

Author: Michelle Mackay
Series Consultant: Carol Lyon
Series Editor: Craig Lowther

© 2024 Leckie

001/10102024

10 9 8 7 6 5 4 3 2 1

ISBN 9780008680305

Published by
Leckie
An imprint of HarperCollins Publishers
Westerhill Road, Bishopbriggs, Glasgow, G64 2QT

T: 0844 576 8126 F: 0844 576 8131
leckiescotland@harpercollins.co.uk www.leckiescotland.co.uk

HarperCollins Publishers
Macken House, 39/40 Mayor Street Upper, Dublin 1, D01 C9W8, Ireland

Publisher: Fiona McGlade

Special thanks
Project editor: Peter Dennis
Layout: Siliconchips
Proofreader: Julianna Dunn

A CIP Catalogue record for this book is available from the British Library.

Acknowledgements
Images © Shutterstock.com

Whilst every effort has been made to trace the copyright holders, in cases where this has been unsuccessful, or if any have inadvertently been overlooked, the Publishers would gladly receive any information enabling them to rectify any error or omission at the first opportunity.

Printed in the UK by Martins the Printers

This book contains FSC™ certified paper and other controlled sources to ensure responsible forest management.

For more information visit: www.harpercollins.co.uk/green

Contents

Answers
Check your answers to this workbook online: https://collins.co.uk/pages/scottish-primary-maths

5.1 Making and naming equal parts

1 Tick the shapes that have been split into **equal** parts.

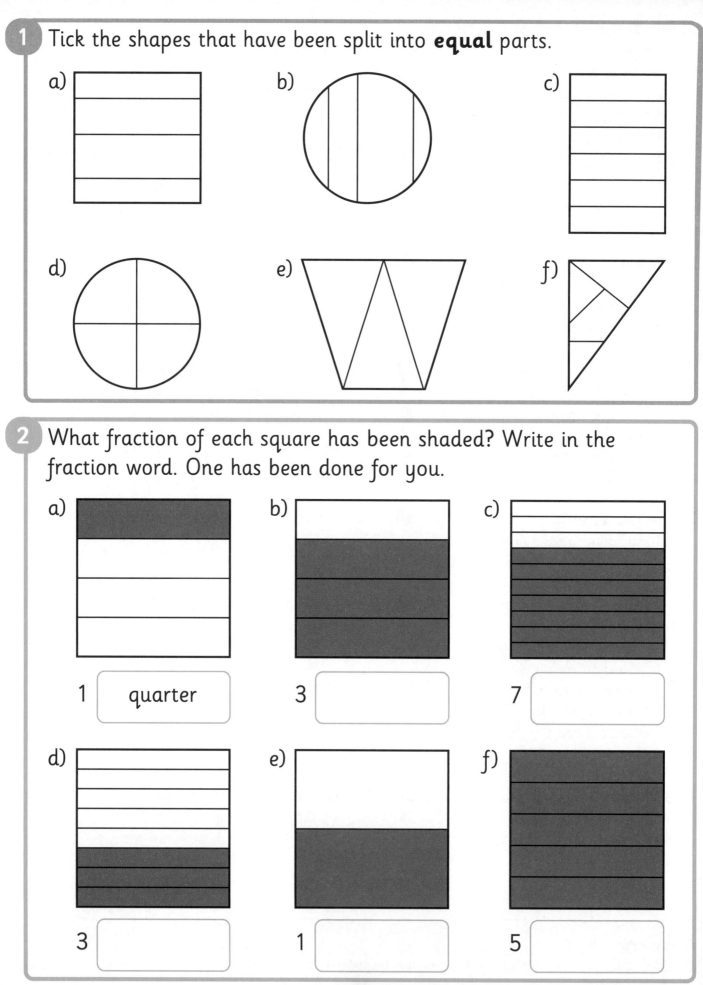

a)

b)

c)

d)

e)

f)

2 What fraction of each square has been shaded? Write in the fraction word. One has been done for you.

a)

1 | quarter

b)

3 |

c)

7 |

d)

3 |

e)

1 |

f)

5 |

a) Draw 4 squares. Split each square into halves.
Each square should be halved in a different way.

b) Draw 4 more squares. Split each square into quarters.
Each square should be quartered in a different way.

c) Draw 2 rectangles. Split each rectangle into quarters.
Each rectangle should be quartered a different way.

5.2 Identifying equal parts

1 Some of each chocolate bar has been eaten. What fraction of each bar is left? The first one has been done for you.

a)

| one eighth | left |

b)

| | left |

c)

| | left |

d)

| | left |

e)

| | left |

f)

| | left |

2 What fraction has been shaded in each of these diagrams? Write your answers in words. The first one has been done for you.

a)

| one quarter |

b)

| |

c)

| |

d)

| |

e)

| |

f)

| |

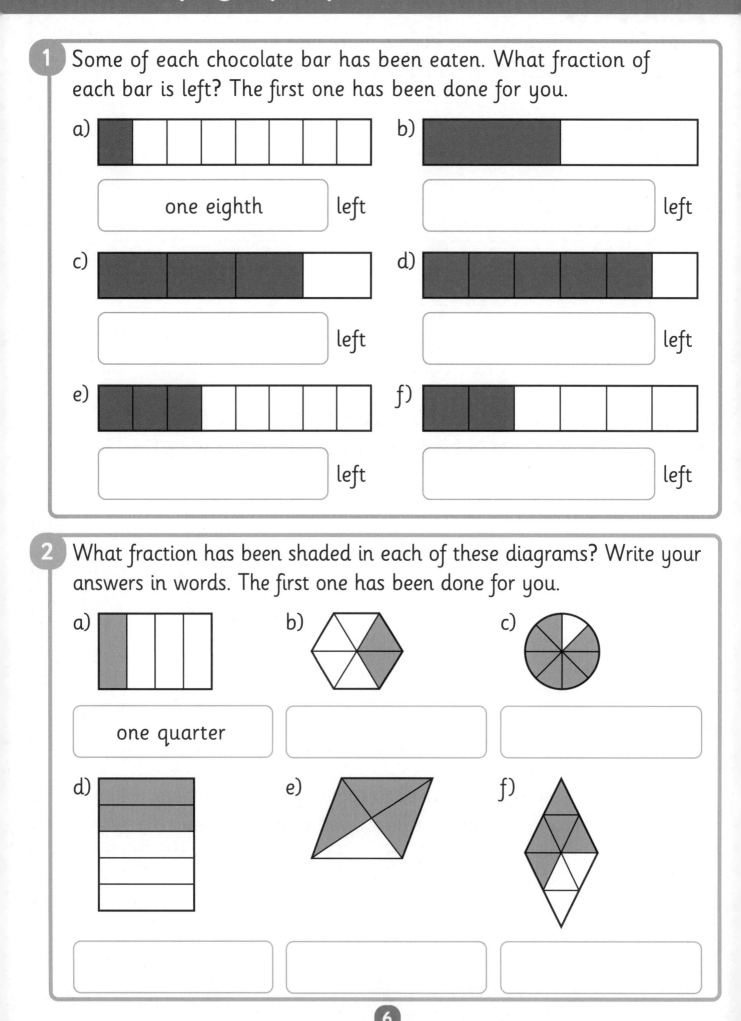

3 Complete the bar to show the following fractions. The first one has been done for you.

a) three sixths

b) four sixths

c) two thirds

d) two quarters

e) seven eighths

f) three thirds

★ **Challenge**

Finlay has drawn three squares. He thinks he has split each one into quarters.

a) Explain to Finlay why he is wrong.

b) Draw two different shapes of your own. Split each one into eighths.

1 What fraction is shaded? Write your answers in words and numbers. The first one has been done for you.

a)

| 2 | out of | 6 | equal parts | two sixths | $\frac{2}{6}$ |

b)

| | out of | | equal parts | | |

c)

| | out of | | equal parts | | |

d)

| | out of | | equal parts | | |

e)

| | out of | | equal parts | | |

f)

| | out of | | equal parts | | |

2 Draw bars and colour the parts to show the following fractions. The first one has been done for you.

a) $\frac{3}{6}$ b) $\frac{3}{4}$

c) $\frac{5}{8}$

d) $\frac{1}{6}$

e) $\frac{2}{3}$

f) $\frac{5}{5}$

3 What fraction has **not** been coloured for each of your answers in Question 2. Write your answers in numbers and words. One has been done for you.

a) $\boxed{\frac{3}{6}}$ three sixths

b) $\boxed{}$

c) $\boxed{}$

d) $\boxed{}$

e) $\boxed{}$

f) $\boxed{}$

★ **Challenge**

Match the fraction with the correct number of wholes and parts. One has been done for you.

$\frac{6}{2}$

$\frac{9}{7}$

$\frac{5}{4}$

$\frac{5}{3}$

$\frac{8}{5}$

$\frac{8}{6}$

One whole and one quarter

Three wholes

One whole and two sixths

One whole and three fifths

One whole and two thirds

One whole and two sevenths

5.4 Counting fractions

1 Complete the empty boxes on the number sticks. The first one has been done for you.

a) Halves

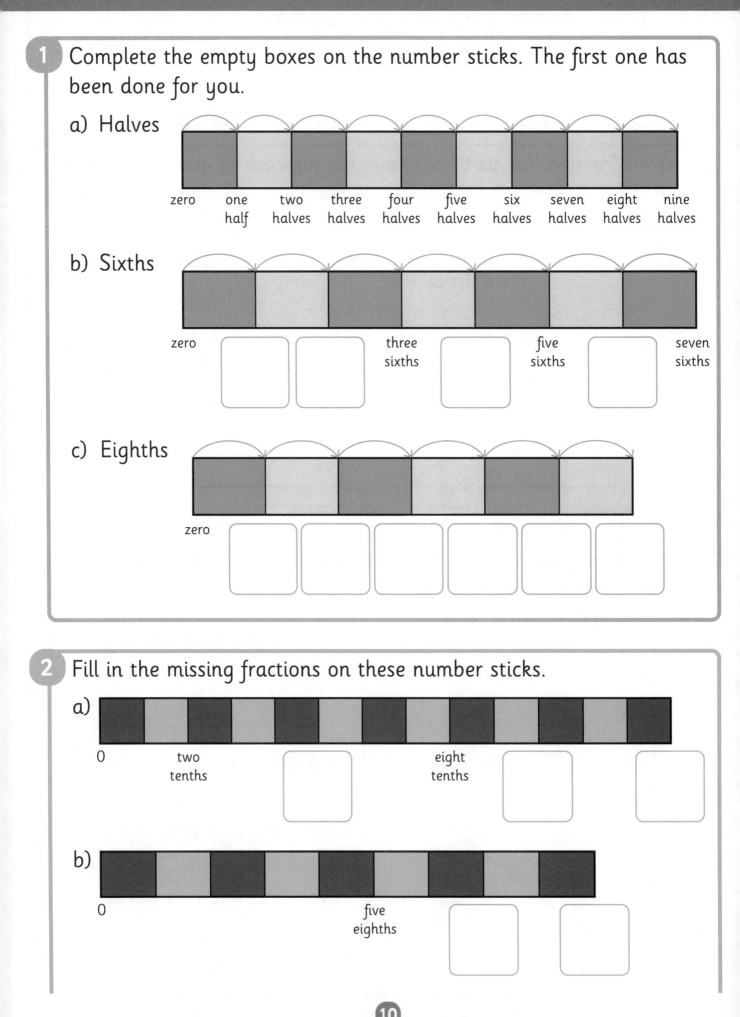

| zero | one half | two halves | three halves | four halves | five halves | six halves | seven halves | eight halves | nine halves |

b) Sixths

| zero | | | three sixths | | five sixths | | seven sixths |

c) Eighths

zero

2 Fill in the missing fractions on these number sticks.

a)

0   two tenths   eight tenths

b)

0   five eighths

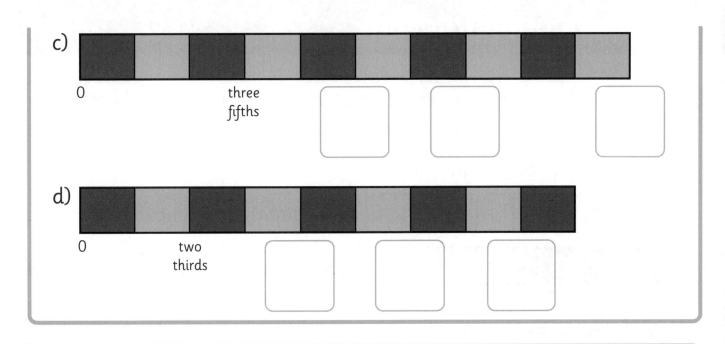

c)

0   three   ▢   ▢   ▢
           fifths

d)

0   two   ▢   ▢   ▢
           thirds

---

3 Finlay notices there are 13 tenths in Question 2a). He knows 10 tenths equals 1 whole, so 13 tenths is the same as 1 whole and 3 tenths.

Write the largest fraction from each number stick in Question 2 as wholes and fraction parts. One has been done for you.

a)
> 1 whole and 3 tenths

b)
>

c)
>

d)
>

★ **Challenge**

Write these fractions in the correct place on the number line:

$\frac{4}{4}$ $\frac{8}{4}$ $\frac{1}{4}$ $\frac{5}{4}$ $\frac{2}{4}$

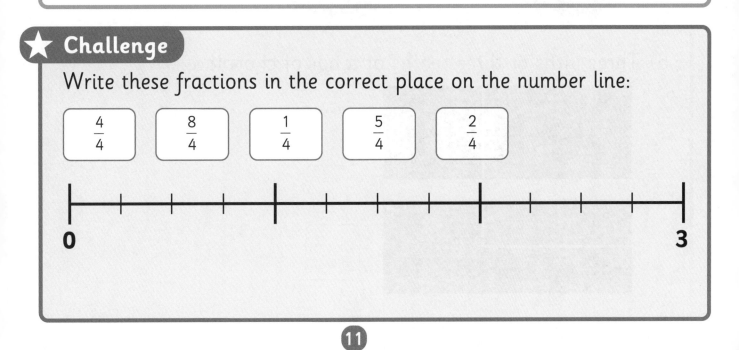

0   3

1 Use cubes to help you work out which is larger, then circle the larger fraction. One has been done for you.

a) 3 eighths **or** (4 eighths)

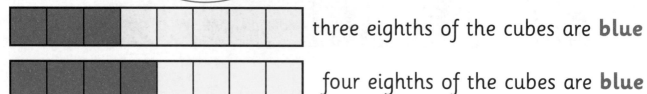 three eighths of the cubes are **blue**

four eighths of the cubes are **blue**

b) 5 tenths **or** 7 tenths

c) 5 sixths **or** 4 sixths

d) 5 twelfths **or** 8 twelfths

e) 5 sevenths **or** 3 sevenths

2 Tick the smaller fraction:

a) Two sixths or two thirds of a cake

b) Three fifths or three tenths of a bar of chocolate.

3 Circle the correct answer, True or False.

a)

Four sevenths

Five sixths

Five sixths is larger than four sevenths.

True   False

b)

Three eighths

Seven tenths

Three eighths is larger than seven tenths.

True   False

c)

Two thirds

Four sixths

Four sixths is smaller than two thirds.

True   False

d)

Five fifths

Nine tenths

Five fifths is smaller than nine tenths.

True   False

★ Challenge

Nuria ate $\frac{2}{8}$ of a pizza.

a) Write as many fractions as you can that are smaller than $\frac{2}{8}$.

b) Write as many fractions as you can that are larger than $\frac{2}{8}$.

5.6 Equivalent fractions

1 Draw lines to match the fractions that are equivalent (of equal size).

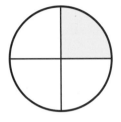
one quarter

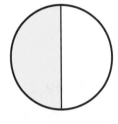
one half

two sixths

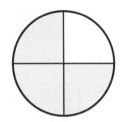
three quarters

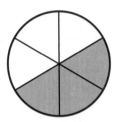
three sixths

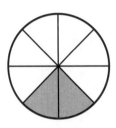
two eighths

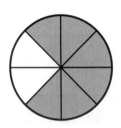
six eighths

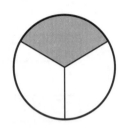
one third

2 a) Draw lines to show matching fractions.

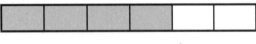
four sixths $\frac{4}{6}$

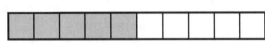
five tenths $\frac{5}{10}$

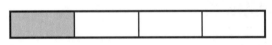
one quarter $\frac{1}{4}$

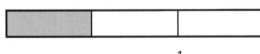
one third $\frac{1}{3}$

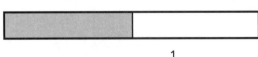
one half $\frac{1}{2}$

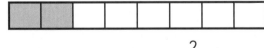
two eighths $\frac{2}{8}$

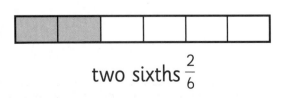
two sixths $\frac{2}{6}$

b) Draw a matching fraction for the fraction that has not been used.

Finlay cuts his pizza into 6 equal slices and Isla cuts her pizza into 8 equal slices.

1. a) Draw lines to divide Finlay's pizza into six equal slices.

   b) Shade **half** of Finlay's pizza. How many sixths is this? Write your answer in words and as a fraction.

2. a) Draw lines to divide Isla's pizza into eight equal slices.

   b) Shade **half** of Isla's pizza. How many eighths is this? Write your answer in words and as a fraction.

5.7 Counting in fractions

1 Fill in the missing numbers on the counting sticks.

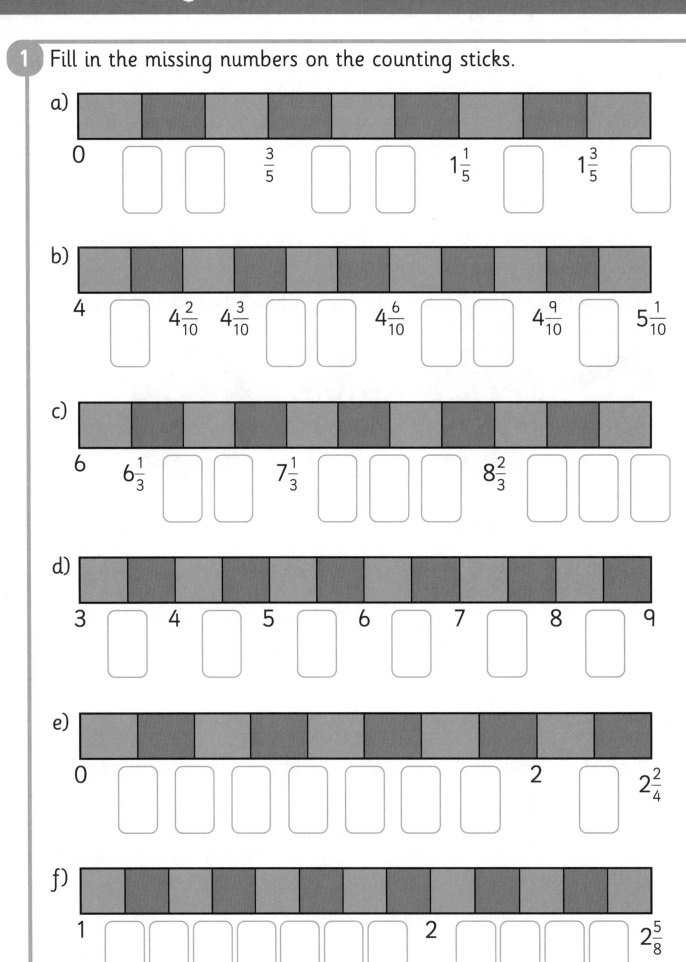

a) 0 ☐ ☐ $\frac{3}{5}$ ☐ ☐ $1\frac{1}{5}$ ☐ $1\frac{3}{5}$ ☐

b) 4 ☐ $4\frac{2}{10}$ $4\frac{3}{10}$ ☐ ☐ $4\frac{6}{10}$ ☐ ☐ $4\frac{9}{10}$ ☐ $5\frac{1}{10}$

c) 6 $6\frac{1}{3}$ ☐ ☐ $7\frac{1}{3}$ ☐ ☐ ☐ $8\frac{2}{3}$ ☐ ☐ ☐

d) 3 ☐ 4 ☐ 5 ☐ 6 ☐ 7 ☐ 8 ☐ 9

e) 0 ☐ ☐ ☐ ☐ ☐ ☐ ☐ 2 ☐ $2\frac{2}{4}$

f) 1 ☐ ☐ ☐ ☐ ☐ ☐ ☐ 2 ☐ ☐ ☐ ☐ $2\frac{5}{8}$

2 Draw a number stick that counts on from:

a) 0 to 1 in jumps of one quarter.

b) 0 to 1 in jumps of one third.

c) 0 to 1 in jumps of one fifth.

★ **Challenge**

Some numbers have fallen off the number sticks. Help Finlay put them back in the correct places.

| 0 | | $\frac{2}{3}$ | 1 | $1\frac{1}{3}$ | $1\frac{2}{3}$ | | | $2\frac{2}{3}$ | 3 | |

Loose number tokens:

2   $5\frac{3}{4}$ $2\frac{1}{3}$ $6\frac{1}{4}$ $\frac{1}{3}$ 7 $3\frac{1}{3}$

| 5 | $5\frac{1}{4}$ | $5\frac{2}{4}$ | | 6 | | $6\frac{2}{4}$ | $6\frac{3}{4}$ | | $7\frac{1}{4}$ | $7\frac{2}{4}$ |

1 Find the following:

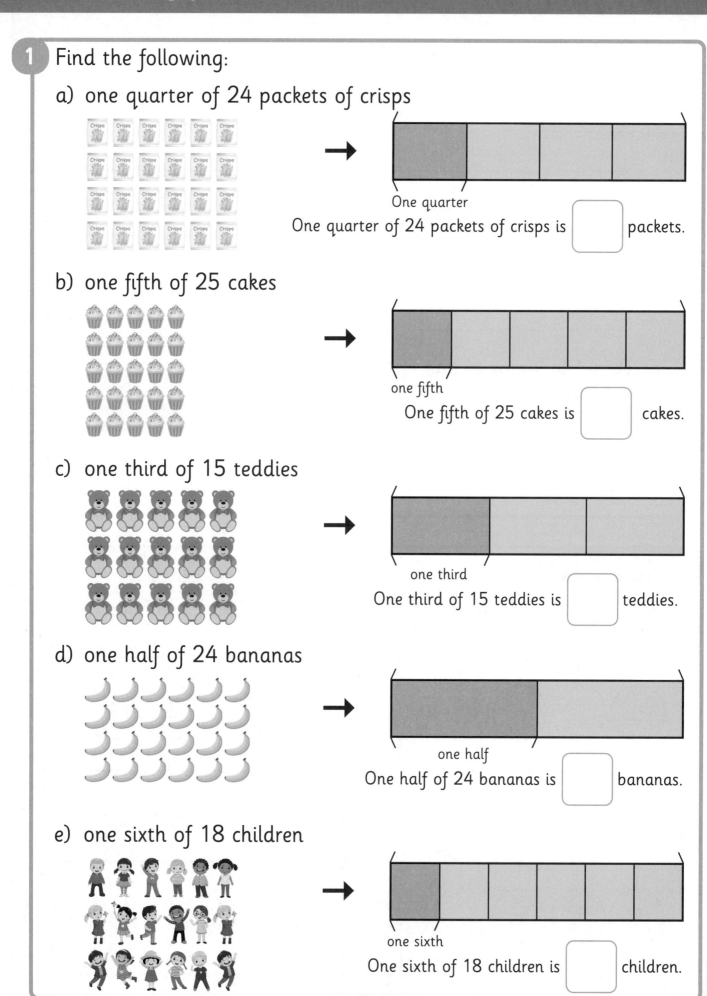

a) one quarter of 24 packets of crisps

One quarter

One quarter of 24 packets of crisps is ☐ packets.

b) one fifth of 25 cakes

one fifth

One fifth of 25 cakes is ☐ cakes.

c) one third of 15 teddies

one third

One third of 15 teddies is ☐ teddies.

d) one half of 24 bananas

one half

One half of 24 bananas is ☐ bananas.

e) one sixth of 18 children

one sixth

One sixth of 18 children is ☐ children.

2 Draw bar models to help you solve these problems.

a) Finlay had 20 cookies. He ate one fifth of them.
How many cookies did Finlay eat?

b) Isla had 40 stickers. She gave away one tenth of them.
How many stickers did Isla give away?

c) Amman had £30. He spent one third of it on a birthday present for his mum. How much did Amman spend on his mum's birthday present?

Write your own story problem using the numbers 16 and one quarter.

Swap story problems with a partner. Can your partner solve your story problem? Can you solve their story problem?

6.1 Making and recording amounts

1 Write these amounts in pence. One has been done for you.

a) £5 and 99p | 599p | b) £6 and 78p | _____ p

c) £5 and 60p | _____ p | d) £1 and 6p | _____ p

e) £4 and 9p | _____ p | f) £9 | _____ p

2 Write these amounts in pounds and pence. One has been done for you.

a) 456p | £4 and 56p | b) 777p | _____

c) 307p | _____ | d) 980p | _____

3 Write each amount in pounds and pence.

a)

b)

4 Write these amounts in pence.

a)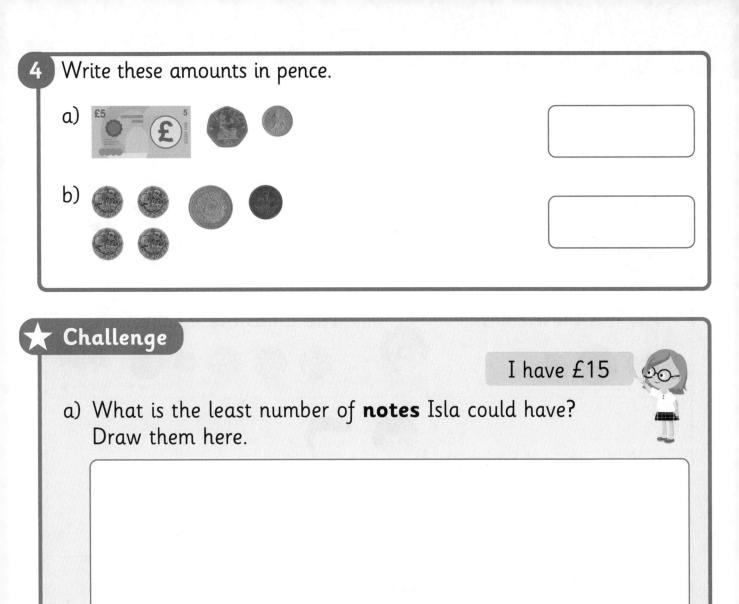

b)

⭐ **Challenge**

I have £15

a) What is the least number of **notes** Isla could have?
   Draw them here.

b) What is the least number of **coins** Isla could have?
   Draw them here.

c) Use notes and coins to find different ways to make £15.
   How many different ways can you find?

1 Together, how much money does each pair of children have? Write your answers in pence.

Amman has these coins:

Finlay has these coins:

Isla has these coins:

Nuria has these coins:

a) Amman and Finlay?

b) Finlay and Nuria?

c) Isla and Amman?

d) Isla and Nuria?

2 The children each have £1 to spend in Joe's shop. Look at what the children want to buy and tick **yes** if they have enough money and **no** if they don't.

Joe's Shop Menu

CRISPS	JUICE		APPLE	CHOCO	COMIC
30p	50p	25p	16p	33p	64p

a) Amman wants:

Does he have enough money to buy both?

Yes ☐ No ☐

b) Isla wants:

Does she have enough money to buy both?

Yes ☐ No ☐

c) Finlay wants:

Does he have enough money to buy all three?

Yes ☐ No ☐

d) Nuria wants:

Does she have enough money to buy all three?

Yes ☐ No ☐

3 Look at your answers for Question 2.

a) Who has enough money to buy what they want?
How much change will they each get from £1?

Name: [   ] Change from £1 [   ]

Name: [   ] Change from £1 [   ]

Name: [   ] Change from £1 [   ]

b) Who does not have enough money? How much **more** does this person need?

[   ] needs [   ]

⭐ **Challenge**

a) Draw 5 things you might buy at a car boot sale. Give each item a different price (between 20p and £1).

[   ]

b) Ask a partner to choose 2 or 3 different items and calculate how much the things would cost in total.

[   ]

c) If your partner paid using a £5 note how much change would they get?

[   ]

6.3 Calculating change

1 Use the number lines (counting up) to work out your change from £1 when you spend these amounts.

a) 35p |————————————————|

b) 7p |————————————————|

c) 64p |————————————————|

d) 41p |————————————————|

2 The children have each been given £2 to spend at the School Fair.

a) Calculate the total cost of the toys they each choose.

School Fair Toy Shop

Stickers	Ball	Yo-yo	Walkie Talkie	Toy Man	Toy car
58p	27p	39p	87p	15p	15p

Isla buys:

and

Total cost:

Nuria buys:

and

Total cost:

Finlay buys:

and

Total cost:

Amman buys:

and

Total cost:

b) How much will each child have left to spend? Show each calculation on the empty number lines.

Isla:

Nuria:

Finlay:

Amman:

a) Isla paid 39p for a packet of crisps, 40p for sweets and 55p for juice.

How much money does Isla need to be able to buy all three items?

b) Isla gives the shopkeeper a £5 note. Show Isla's change in three different ways.

7.1 Time word problems

Solve these problems. Show your working.

1 Amman and Isla are building the same model car from bricks. Amman built his model car in 3 weeks, Isla built her model car in 35 days.

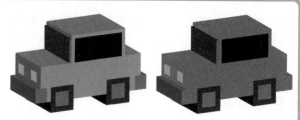

a) Who made their model in the shorter time?

b) How much shorter was this?

2 Olivia's rabbit is 72 months old. Lucy's dog is 84 months old.

How many **years** older is Lucy's dog than Olivia's rabbit?

3 Finlay played for the school football team for 24 months and Amman played for 106 weeks.

a) Who played for the team the longest?

b) How much longer was this?

4 Joe is 12 months old. How old will he be in 12 months' time?

Write your answer in years.

5 Nuria had soup, pizza and dessert for dinner. Nuria ate her dinner in 20 minutes. She ate her soup in 5 minutes and her dessert in 5 minutes.

Menu
(Tick what you want for dinner)

Nuria

Soup ✓   Carrotsticks

Nuggets   Pizza ✓

Dessert ✓   Milkshake

How long did it take Nuria to eat her pizza?

 Challenge

 180 minutes is the same as three hours.

120 hours is the same as 6 days.

a) Is Amman correct? Explain how you know.

b) Is Finlay correct? Explain how you know.

7.2 Finding durations

1 Isla's family stayed at a campsite from Friday to Tuesday. They then travelled in a campervan from Wednesday until the following Tuesday.

a) For how many days did Isla's family stay at the campsite?

b) For how many days were they travelling in a campervan?

c) How many days were the family on holiday for altogether?

2 Nuria went to a netball camp from 14th April to 27th April.

APRIL

Sun	Mon	Tue	Wed	Thu	Fri	Sat
	1	2	3	4	5	6
7	8	9	10	11	12	13
14	15	16	17	18	19	20
21	22	23	24	25	26	27
28	29	30				

a) How many days was Nuria away for?

b) How many weeks was she away for?

3 a) How many days are there in four weeks?

b) How many weeks are in 35 days?

c) How many months are there in a year?

d) How many months are there in four years?

Isla goes to swimming lessons every Monday and every Friday. Her mum pays for 20 lessons.

a) How many weeks will Isla have swimming lessons for?

b) Each lesson lasts 2 hours. How many hours of swimming will Isla have done over the 20 lessons?

c) Isla's lessons started on 8th January 2024. There were no lessons between the 4th March and 17th March because the swimming teacher was on holiday. What date did Isla's 20 lessons end on?

7.3 Recording time

1 a) Use a timer to time how long it takes you to lay out five rows of six counters.
How long did you take?

b) Now jump on the spot for the length of time it took you to lay out the counters. Count your jumps.
How many jumps did you do?

2 a) Estimate how long it will take you to lay out ten rows of three counters.

b) Use a timer to time how long it takes to lay out ten rows of three counters.
How long did it take?

c) Now jump on the spot for the length of time it took you to lay out the counters. Count your jumps.
How many jumps did you do?

3 Use a timer to time how long it takes you to do each activity. Record the time beside each activity.

Activity	Time taken
Hop on one leg 20 times	
Jump on the spot 20 times	
Touch your knees then your toes 25 times	
Do 20 star jumps	
Draw a circle, a square and a triangle	

Activity	Time taken
Count from 1 to 30 out loud	
Say your name 10 times	
Write your name 10 times	

a) What did you use to time the activities?

b) Which activity took the longest amount of time?

c) Which activity took the shortest amount of time?

★ Challenge

a) Choose one of the activities from Question 3. Time yourself doing the activity for exactly one minute. How many times did you manage to do the task in one minute?

b) Choose a different activity from the list and time yourself doing it for one minute. How many times did you manage to do this task in one minute?

c) Which task did you do most times in one minute?
   Why do you think this is?

7.4 Telling the time

1 Draw the hands on each clock face to show the time given.

a)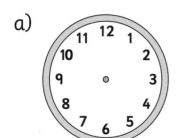

2 o'clock

b)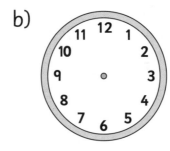

12 o'clock

c)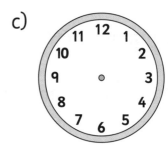

6 o'clock

d)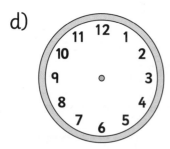

half past 6

e)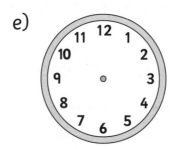

half past 8

f)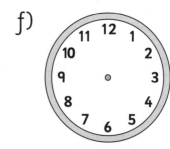

half past 1

g)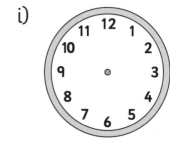

quarter past 2

h) quarter to 4

i) quarter to 6

j)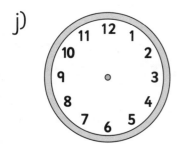

quarter to 12

k) quarter to 3

l)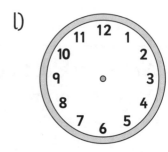

quarter past 1

2 Draw lines to match each analogue time with the equivalent digital time and words.

quarter past 6

quarter to 11

quarter past 8

★ **Challenge**

a) Draw an hour hand and a minute hand on each of these clocks to make two **different** times.

b) Write the time on each clock in words.

c) Now show the same two times on these digital clocks.

:   :

1 Write the time shown on each clock in words.

a)

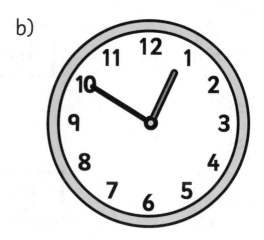

b)

_____

c)

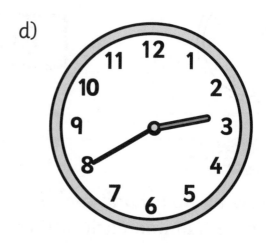

d)

_____

e)

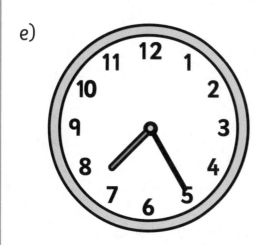

f)

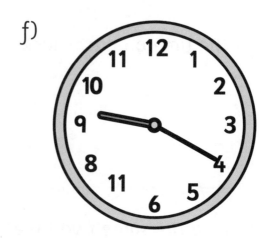

_____

2 Draw the hands on each clock face to show the time given.

a)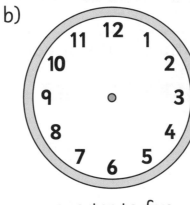

ten minutes past six

b)

quarter to five

c)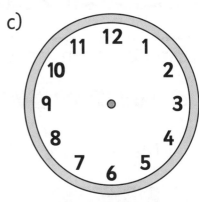

twenty minutes to ten

d)

quarter past seven

e)

twenty-five minutes past four

f)

five minutes to one

★ **Challenge**

Finlay left his house at eight thirty to walk to school.

He took twenty minutes to walk there.

a) Show the time he arrived at school on the clock below.

b) Write this time in words.

1 Estimate then measure the length of each bar in centimetres.

a)

My estimate _____ My measurement _____

b)

My estimate _____ My measurement _____

c)

My estimate _____ My measurement _____

d)

My estimate _____ My measurement _____

2 Use a ruler to draw lines that measure exactly:

a) 4 cm

b) 8 cm

c) 2 cm

d) 10 cm

Find things that you estimate will measure the lengths given in the table. Use a ruler to measure each object. One has been done for you.

Find an object that is about:	Object	Actual measurement
10 cm long	pencil	12 cm
25 cm long		
40 cm long		
70 cm long		
100 cm long		

1 Write down the mass of each object.

a)

pencil case

b)

plant

c)

trainers

d)

lunchbox

2 The pan balances show the mass of a bottle, a lunchbox and a schoolbag.

List the objects in order from lightest to heaviest. Explain your thinking.

Amman and Isla were measuring the mass of different items using a pan balance.

a) Circle the weights Amman will need to add to the empty pan so that it balances.

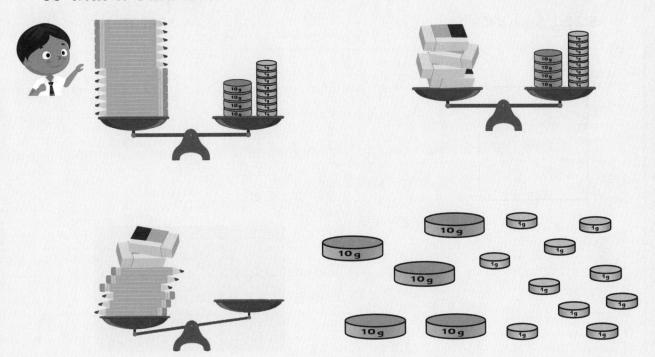

b) Circle the weights Isla will need to add to the empty pan to balance one apple and three bananas.

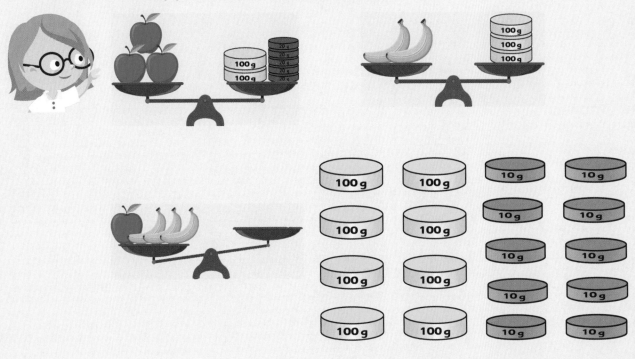

1 Draw the following shapes on the squared grid. Keep the outline of each shape on the lines, like in the yellow square.

a) a different sized square   b) a rectangle   c) a cross   d) a different sized rectangle

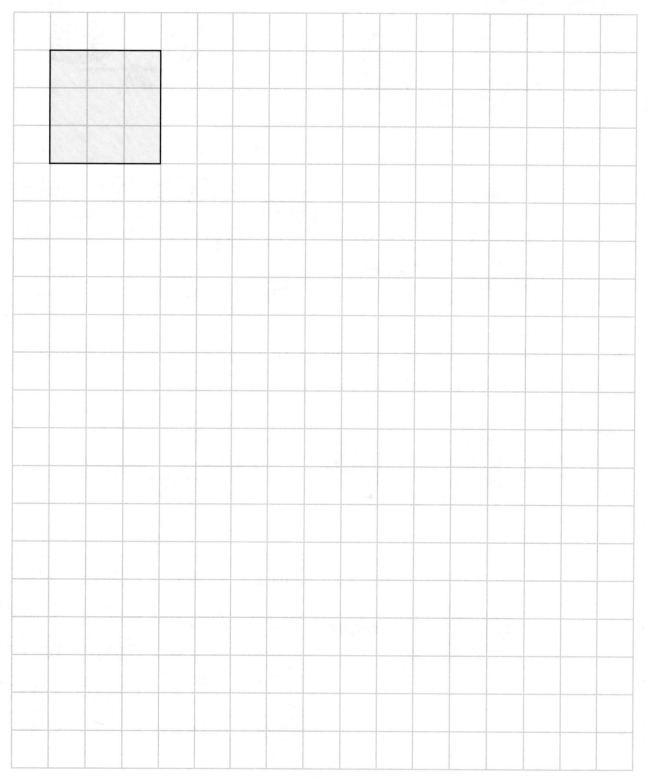

2 The yellow square has an area of 9 squares.

Write down the area of each shape you have drawn.

a) My square has an area of

b) My first rectangle has an area of

c) My cross has an area of

d) My second rectangle has an area of

⭐ **Challenge**

Draw as many different shapes as you can, each with an area of **exactly** 16 squares.

1 Estimate which containers will hold more than 1 litre and which will hold less than 1 litre. Tick 'More than 1 litre' or 'Less than 1 litre' for each one.

a)

can of soup

More than 1 litre	
Less than 1 litre	

b)

can of lemonade

More than 1 litre	
Less than 1 litre	

c)

carton of orange juice

More than 1 litre	
Less than 1 litre	

d)

take-away coffee cup

More than 1 litre	
Less than 1 litre	

e)

bottle of cola

More than 1 litre	
Less than 1 litre	

f)

ladle

More than 1 litre	
Less than 1 litre	

2 What unit of measurement would you use to measure the capacity of each of these, litres or millilitres? Tick litres or millilitres for each container.

a)

tomato sauce bottle

Litres	
Millilitres	

b)

ladle

Litres	
Millilitres	

c)

tin of paint

Litres	
Millilitres	

d)

water jug

Litres	
Millilitres	

e)

bath tub

Litres	
Millilitres	

f)

flower vase

Litres	
Millilitres	

★ **Challenge**

a) Match each container to the most likely capacity.

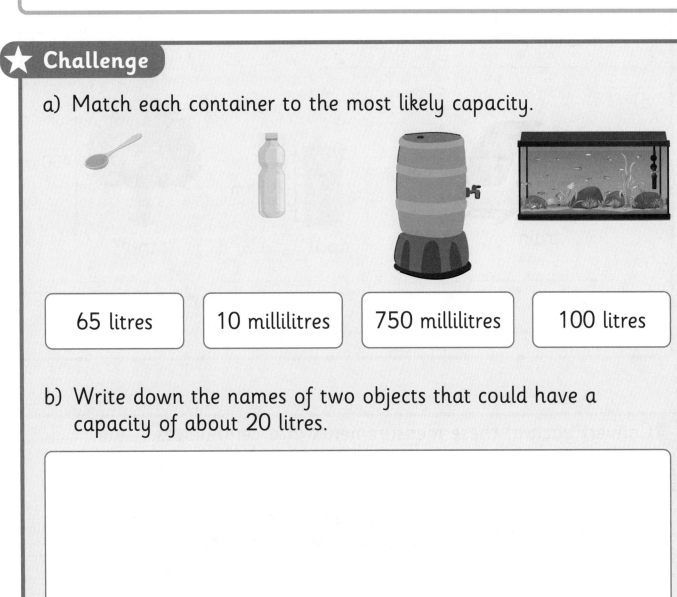

| 65 litres | 10 millilitres | 750 millilitres | 100 litres |

b) Write down the names of two objects that could have a capacity of about 20 litres.

Share your ideas with a partner. Do they agree?

1 Write down how tall each object is in metres (m) and centimetres (cm).
One has been done for you.

a)

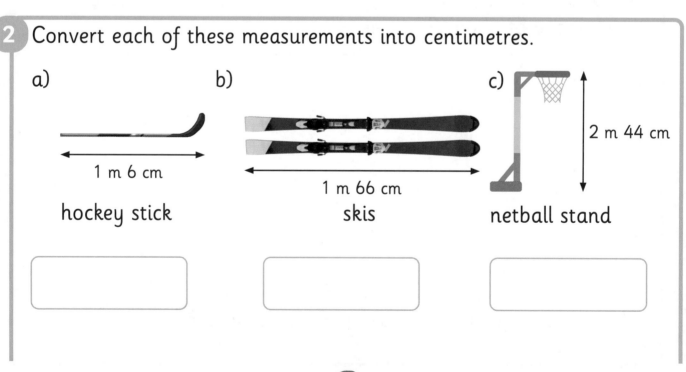

103 cm

bicycle

1 m 3 cm

b)

325 cm

lorry

c)

267 cm

van

d)

398 cm

train

e)

203 cm

door

f)

450 cm

tree

2 Convert each of these measurements into centimetres.

a)

1 m 6 cm

hockey stick

b)

1 m 66 cm

skis

c)

2 m 44 cm

netball stand

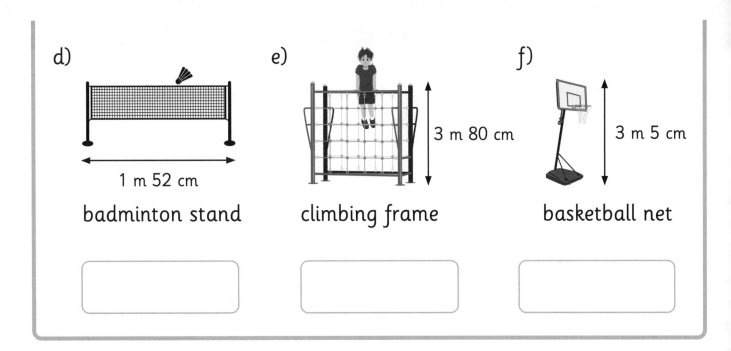

d)

badminton stand

1 m 52 cm

e)

climbing frame

3 m 80 cm

f)

basketball net

3 m 5 cm

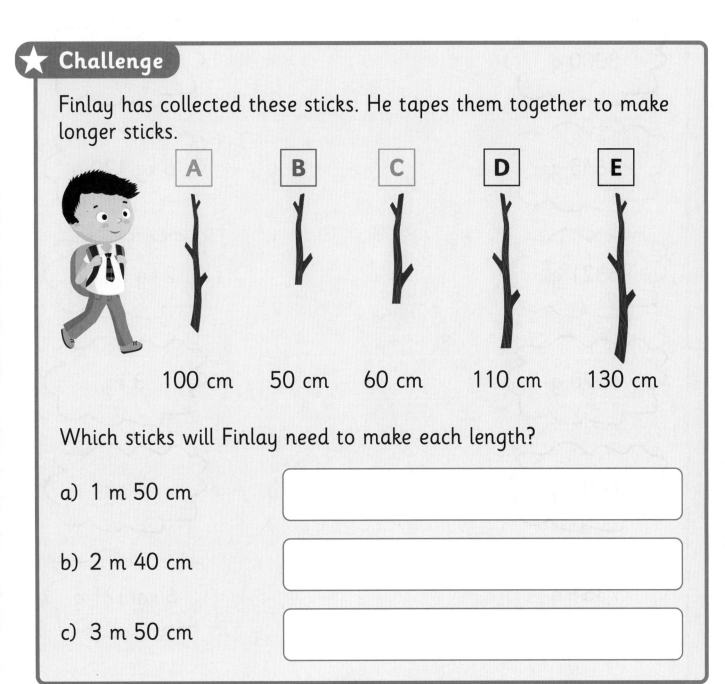

★ Challenge

Finlay has collected these sticks. He tapes them together to make longer sticks.

A   B   C   D   E

100 cm   50 cm   60 cm   110 cm   130 cm

Which sticks will Finlay need to make each length?

a) 1 m 50 cm

b) 2 m 40 cm

c) 3 m 50 cm

1 Match the mass in grams to the correct mass in kilograms and grams. One has been done for you.

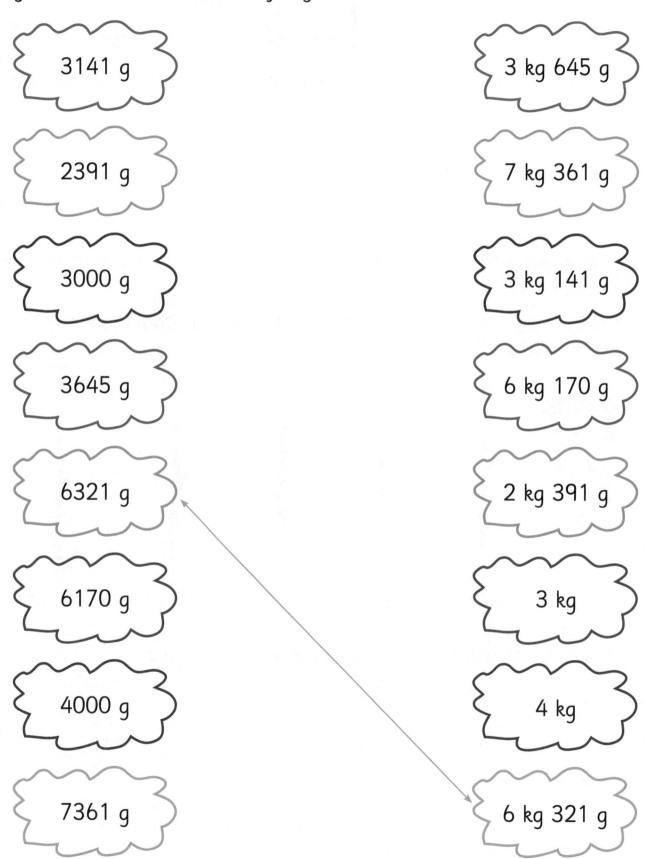

3141 g

2391 g

3000 g

3645 g

6321 g

6170 g

4000 g

7361 g

3 kg 645 g

7 kg 361 g

3 kg 141 g

6 kg 170 g

2 kg 391 g

3 kg

4 kg

6 kg 321 g

2 Write the total mass in kilograms and grams.

a)

b)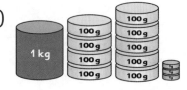

c)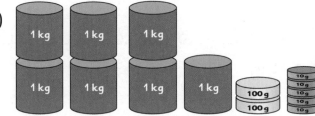

d)

e)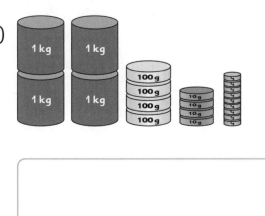

f)

Nuria has a new sand pit in her garden and needs to order sand to fill it.

Sand comes in 4 kg sacks and $2\frac{1}{2}$ kg sacks.

How many of each sack will Nuria need to order to have exactly 18 kg of sand? Explain your thinking.

8.7 Reading scales – length

1 Use a ruler to draw lines that measure:

a) 4 cm

b) 2 cm

c) 9 cm

d) 13 cm

e) 15 cm

f) 11 cm

g) 16 cm

2 Draw lines to match each length in centimetres with the correct length in metres and centimetres. One has been done for you.

 709 cm

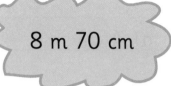 8 m 70 cm

 870 cm

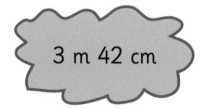 3 m 42 cm

 555 cm

 9 m

 692 cm

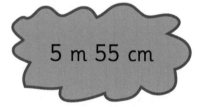 5 m 55 cm

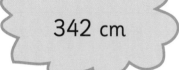 342 cm

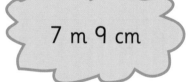 7 m 9 cm

 900 cm

6 m 92 cm

Nuria, Finlay, Amman and Isla all measure the height of Nuria's dog.

I think she is 95 cm tall.

That's far too tall, Finlay. I think she might be 85 cm tall.

I think she is 1 m 5 cm tall.

I think she is 1 m 15 cm tall.

Who is correct? Explain your thinking.

1 Amman, Finlay, Isla and Nuria are going on a day trip.

They each weigh their rucksacks before putting them on the bus.

Write True or False for each statement. Explain your answers to a partner. Do they agree?

	True or False
Isla's bag weighs the least.	
Finlay's bag weighs the most.	
Nuria's bag weighs 5 kg.	
Amman's bag is the heaviest.	
Nuria's bag is the lightest.	

2 Write the mass shown on each scale in kilograms.

a)

b)

c)

d)

e)

f)

⭐ **Challenge**

Finlay and Isla were in the supermarket buying fruit.

Finlay bought some apples.   Isla bought some oranges.

1500 g

Did Finlay's apples weigh more than, less than, or the same as Isla's oranges? Explain your thinking.

8.9 Reading scales – capacity

1 Match the volume of water shown on each jug with the correct measurement. One has been done for you.

a)

400 ml

b)

350 ml

c)

200 ml

d)

50 ml

e)

900 ml

f)

1 litre

g)

650 ml

2 Shade each jug to show the given capacity.

a) 500 ml

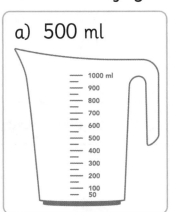

b) 450 ml

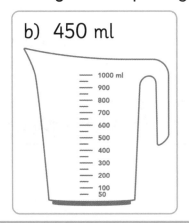

c) 200 ml

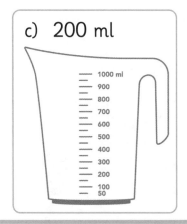

★ **Challenge**

Finlay has four old, different jugs. Parts of the scales have rubbed off!

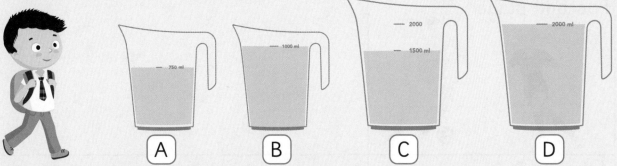

A   B   C   D

He wants to fill the following containers to the top with water. Which measuring jugs could he use?

a)

3 litres

b)

$4\frac{1}{2}$ litres

c)

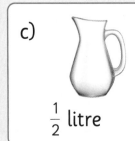

$\frac{1}{2}$ litre

1 Write down some ways that each of these people might use numbers in their jobs.

Job	How numbers are used in this job
Pilot	
Football player	
Joiner	
Scientist	
Shop assistant	

2 **a)** Isla asked her dad about all the different ways numbers are used in his car and when he is driving. Write down all the ways Isla's dad might have told her.

★ **Challenge**

Amman's dad decorates houses. He checks what needs to be done so that he can order the paint and work out the cost.

Amman is thinking about how his dad uses numbers in his work.

Measure the room

How else might Amman's dad use numbers in his work?
Write them in the speech bubble.

10.1 Investigate repeating patterns

1 Continue these patterns.

a)

b)

c)

d)

2 Complete these shape patterns.

a)

b)

c)

d)

3 Complete these repeating patterns by adding the missing shapes.

a) ⬣ ▲ ● ☐ ☐ ☐ ⬣ ☐ ☐ ⬣ ☐

b) ▮ ▬ ● ◣ ☐ ☐ ● ☐ ☐ ☐ ☐

c) ▽ ▬ ■ ☐ ▬ ☐ ☐ ☐ ☐ ☐ ☐

d) ⬠ ● ▲ ☐ ☐ ☐ ⬠ ☐ ☐ ☐ ⬠

⭐ **Challenge**

Isla and Nuria are making patterns using these coloured shapes.

a) Isla creates a pattern that uses 2 different shapes and 4 different colours. What could Isla's pattern be?

b) Nuria's pattern uses only the shapes with exactly 4 sides. What could her pattern be?

1 Complete these patterns.

a)

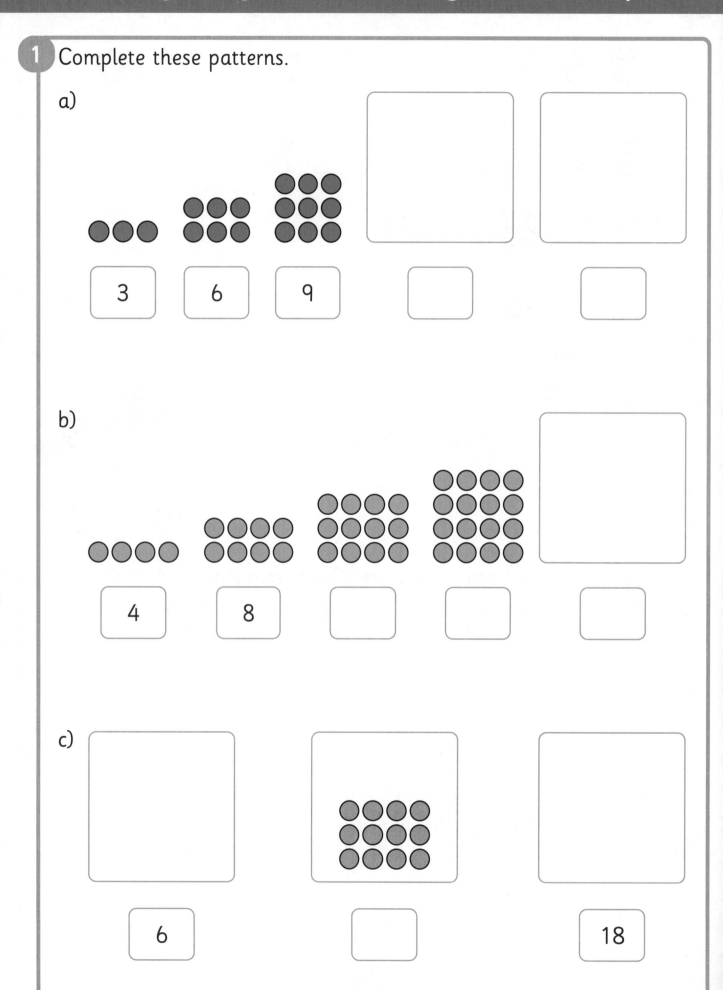

| 3 | 6 | 9 | | |

b)

| 4 | 8 | | | |

c)

| 6 | | 18 |

2 Continue these number patterns:

a) [2], [4], [6], [8], [ ], [ ], [ ]

b) [3], [6], [9], [ ], [ ], [ ], [ ]

c) [0], [5], [ ], [ ], [ ], [25], [30]

d) [110], [120], [130], [ ], [ ], [ ], [ ]

e) [300], [400], [ ], [ ], [ ], [800], [ ]

f) [400], [450], [500], [ ], [ ], [ ], [ ]

★ **Challenge**

a) Help Nuria and Finlay to complete this number sequence.

41 46 51 [ ] [ ] [ ] 71

b) Now make up two number sequences of your own, starting with 41. Swap with a partner. Can you work out what the patterns are?

1

If = 2 and = 4

draw what needs to be added to balance the scales.

a)

b)

c)

d)

2 Find the missing number in these number sentences.

a) 4 + ☐ = 15

b) 20 − ☐ = 5

c) 16 + ☐ = 30

d) 25 − ☐ = 8

e) ☐ + 17 = 25

f) ☐ − 12 = 10

★ **Challenge**

 = 2   ☐ = 5   ◆ = 10

a) Draw these shapes onto the balance, making sure each side equals the same amount. You need to use all of the shapes.

b) Can you find a different way? Remember, you need to use all of the shapes.

12.1 Properties of 2D shapes

1 Complete the table for each shape.

Shape	Name of shape	Number of sides	Number of corners	Fewer than four sides (yes or no)	At least one square corner (yes or no)
	square				
	right-angled triangle				
	rectangle				
	pentagon				
	hexagon				
	triangle (not right-angled)				

2 Match each shape to the statements that could be true for it. One has been done for you.

Triangle   Does not have a right angle

Pentagon   Has 2 sides the same length

Square   Can have 1 right angle

Hexagon   All sides can be a different length

rectangle   Has more than 3 right angles

The picture shows a right-angled triangle and a pentagon.
There are 8 sides and 8 corners altogether.

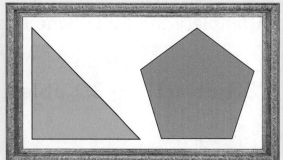

Draw three shapes that together have a total of 11 sides and 11 corners.

12.2 2D shapes in 3D objects

1 Complete the table. One has been done for you.

3D object	Name of 3D object	Number of faces	Number of corners	Number of edges
	cube	6	8	12
	square-based pyramid			
	cuboid			
	cylinder			

2 Finlay and Nuria were building 3D objects in the construction area.

a) Finlay built a pyramid like this.

Which 2D shapes did Finlay use to make his pyramid?
How many of each 2D shape did he need?

Draw or name the shapes he used here.

b) Nuria built a cube like this.

Which 2D shapes did Nuria use to make her cube?
How many of each 2D shape did she need?

Draw or name the shapes she used here.

c) Amman joined Finlay and Nuria. He built a cuboid,
Which 2D shapes do you think he used?

Draw or name the shapes Amman used here.

3 Isla is describing 3D objects by talking about their corners.
Name the 3D objects she could be describing.

a) It has 8 corners.

b) It has no corners.

c) It has 1 corner.

d) It has 5 corners.

Challenge

Can you spot the odd one out? Tick the 3D object that is the odd one out and explain why.

a)

☐   ☐   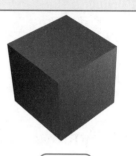☐

b)

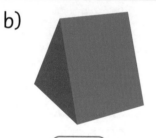

☐   ☐   ☐

c) Now make up your own odd one out question.

1 Draw lines to match each 3D object to its base view. One has been done for you.

2 In each group of 3D objects, two are the same and one is different.
Tick the odd one out each time.

a)

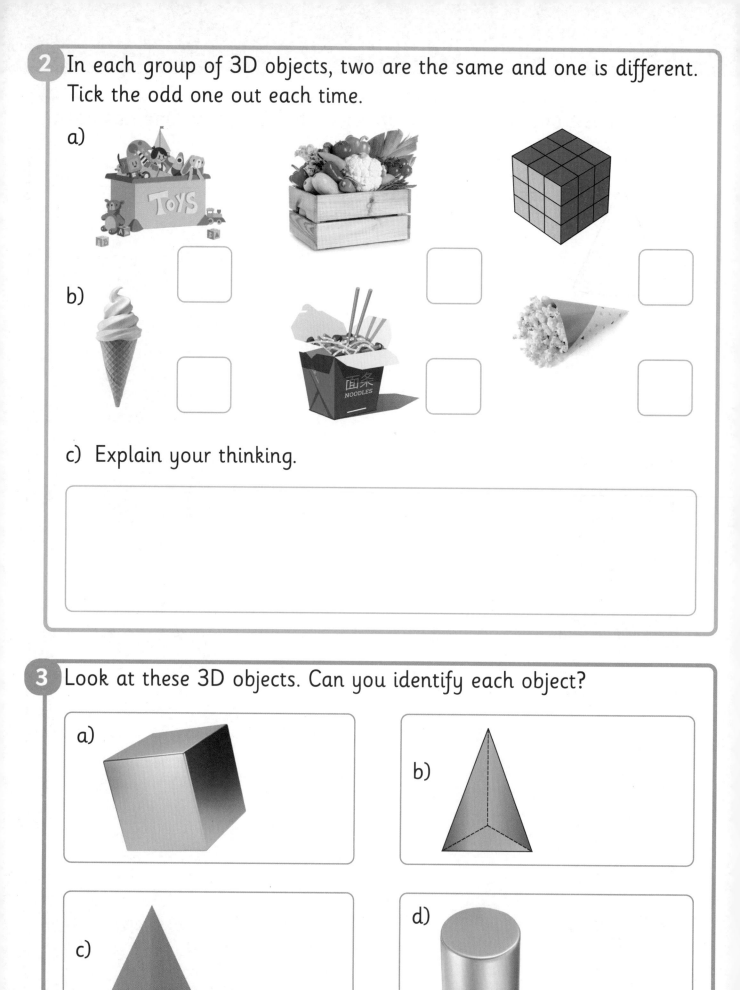

b)

c) Explain your thinking.

3 Look at these 3D objects. Can you identify each object?

a)

b)

c)

d)

Use cubes to make a 3D object.

a) Draw a side view of the object you have made.

b) Now draw your object as if you are looking down on it from above.

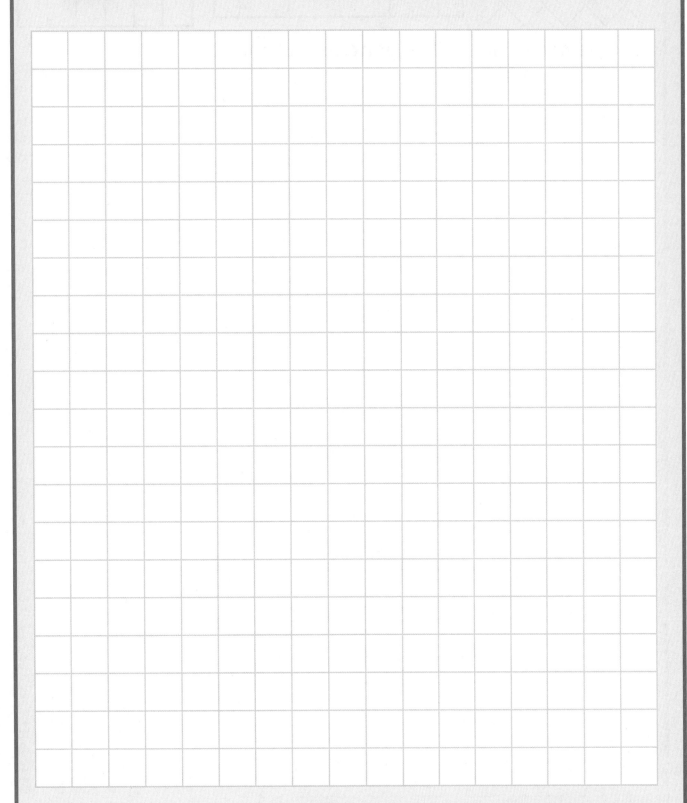

12.4 Tiling patterns

1 Look at these different tiling patterns.

Choose one of these tiling patterns and copy it.

2 Use a 2D shape to create your own tiling pattern.

You could use a square, a rectangle, a triangle or a hexagon.

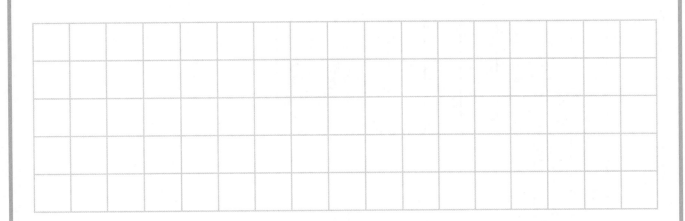

Use a different 2D shape to create a different tiling pattern.
Fill as much of the box as you can with your pattern.

Continue this tiling pattern.

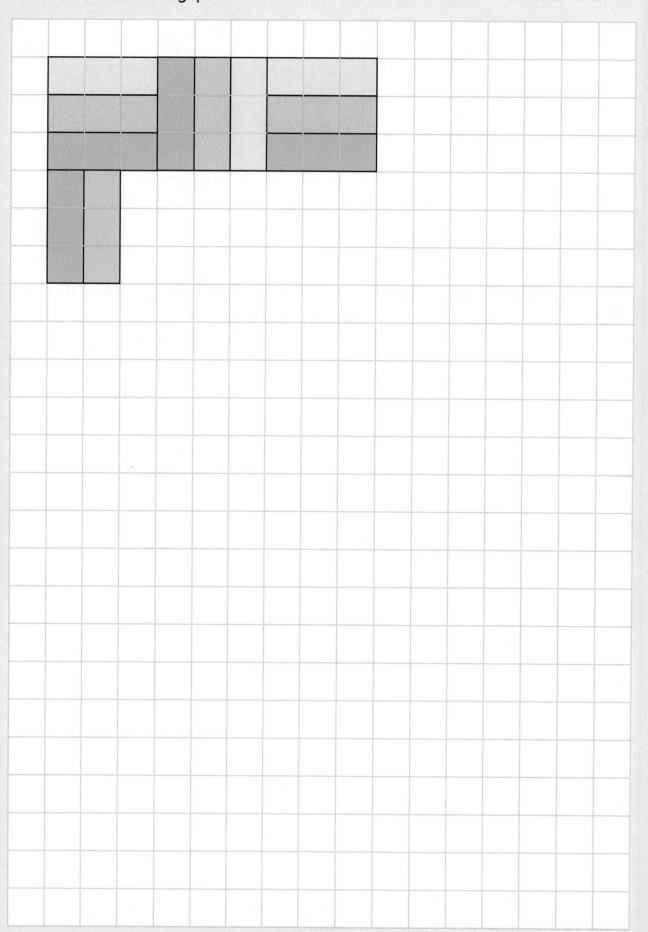

13.1 Making turns

1 These shapes have been turned. Colour the shapes that have made a **full turn** red. Colour the shapes that have made a **half turn** blue.

a)

b)

c)

d)

e)

f)

2 Each of these shapes has made a quarter turn. Colour the shapes that turned **clockwise** green. Colour the shapes that turned **anticlockwise** yellow.

a)

b)

c)

d)

e)

f)

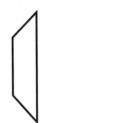

3 Draw these shapes so that they have made the correct turn. You may use tracing paper to help you.

a) quarter turn anti-clockwise

b) half turn

c) full turn

d) quarter turn clockwise

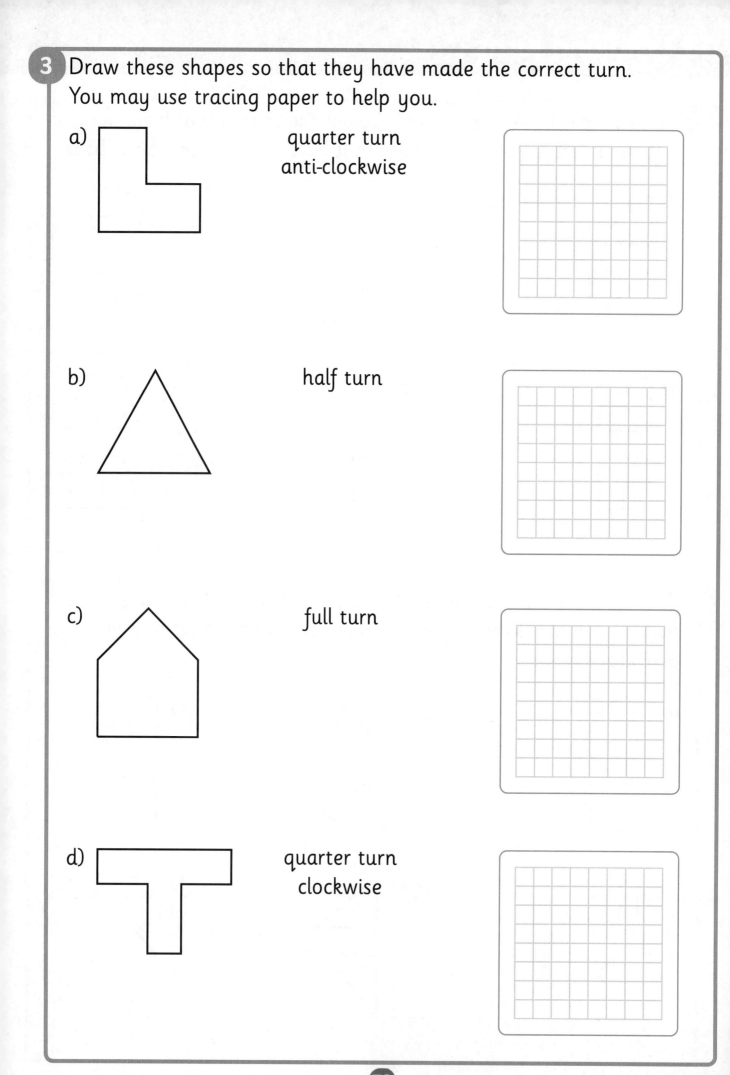

Isla is playing a computer game. She needs to help the cat to catch a mouse.

Draw arrows on the grid to show the cat's journey. ↑ ↓ ← →

- The cat walks six squares to the right and makes a quarter turn clockwise.
- The cat then walks forwards six squares and makes a quarter turn anti-clockwise.
- Next, it walks forwards four squares and makes a quarter turn clockwise.
- After that, it walks five squares and makes a quarter turn anti-clockwise.
- Finally, the cat walks forward two squares.
  Draw a mouse in this square.

1 Tick the objects that have at least one **right angle**. Put a cross beside those with **no** right angles.

a)

☐

b)

☐

c)

☐

d)

☐

e)

☐

f)

☐

2 Find as many right angles as you can in each of these shapes. Write down how many you find for each shape.

Mark the right angles like this: ⌐

a)

☐
right angles

b)

☐
right angles

c)

☐
right angles

d)

☐
right angles

e)

☐
right angles

f)

☐
right angles

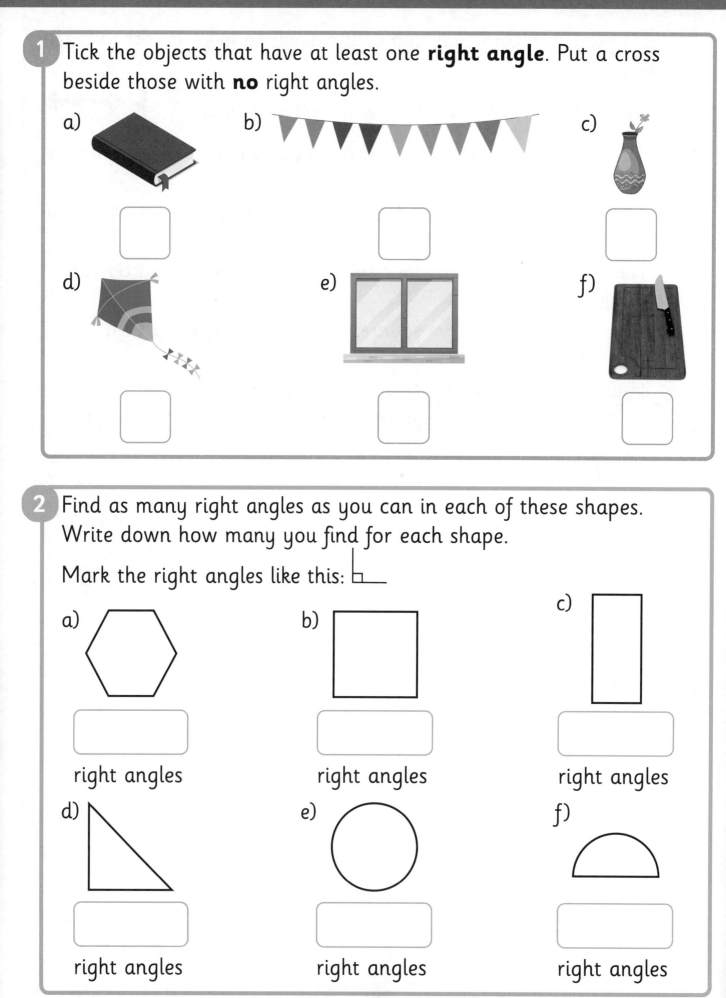

3 a) Draw a shape that has at least 2 right angles.

b) Draw a shape that has exactly 1 right angle.

c) Draw a shape with straight edges and no right angles.

a) Add letters to the table to show where each shape fits.
One has been done for you.

No right angles	One right angle	More than one right angle
F		

b) Draw a new shape that follows each rule.

No right angles	One right angle	More than one right angle

13.3 Grid references

1 Write down the grid references for each shape.
One has been done for you.

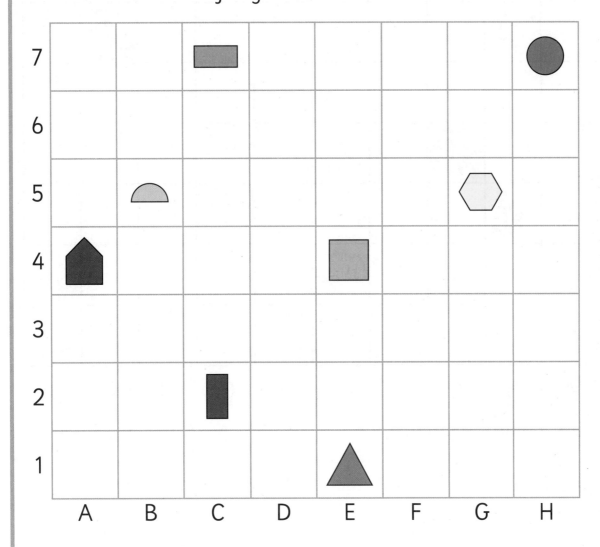

a) ⬤ H7

b) ▢

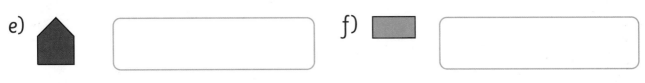

c) ▮

d) ▲

e) ⬠

f) ▬

g) ⬡

h) ◗

2 Finlay has drawn a map of where he lives.

	A	B	C	D	E	F	G	H	I	J
7	Doctors surgery						Amman's house			
6		Shop							Finlay's house	
5										
4			Nuria's house		Church					
3		Isla house								
2	SCHOOL				Park					Castle
1										Pond

a) Write the grid reference for:

Finlay's house [ ]   Shop [ ]

Castle [ ]   School [ ]

Church [ ]   Park [ ]

b) What is at each of these grid references?

B3 [ ]   J1 [ ]

G7 [ ]   E2 [ ]

A7 [ ]   C4 [ ]

a) Complete the table. The first row has been done for you.

Object	Grid reference	Goes with	Grid reference
Beehive	H3	Bee	A7
Flowerpot			
Glass			
Car			

13.4 Symmetry

1 Use a mirror to test each object to see if it is symmetrical.

   a) Tick the objects that are symmetrical and cross the ones that are not.

   b) Draw the line of symmetry on each symmetrical object.

2 a) Use a pencil and a ruler to draw **one** line of symmetry on each shape.

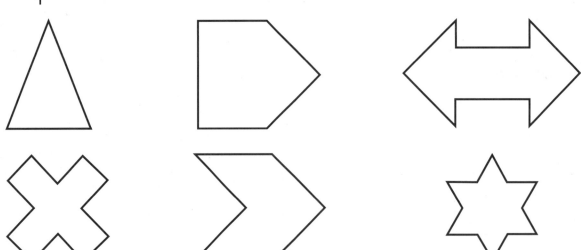

   b) Colour half of each shape.

3 a) Draw a shape with one line of symmetry. Draw the line of symmetry.

b) Draw a shape that has two lines of symmetry. Draw the lines of symmetry.

c) Draw a shape that has more than two lines of symmetry. Draw the lines of symmetry.

The children have lots of shapes like these:

a) Amman creates a symmetrical shape by fitting together 2 rectangles and 2 triangles.

Draw the shape you think Amman built.

b) Isla says she has built a symmetrical shape out of 2 squares, 2 rectangles and 1 triangle.

Finlay says, "But that's impossible." Do you think Finlay is right? Explain your thinking or draw the shape.

1 Nuria completed a survey about sports. Her responses are shown here.

Sports survey

Do you like sports?

☑ Yes   ☐ No

Which sports do you take part in?

☐ swimming   ☐ basketball

☑ dancing   ☐ karate

☑ football   ☐ rounders

Which do you like best?

dancing

a) Does Nuria like sports?

b) Which sports does she **not** do?

c) Which sports does she do?

d) Which sport does she like best?

2 This is a tally of favourite foods at break.

Food	Tally
crisps	卌 卌 II
pizza	III
apple	卌
chocolate	卌 IIII

a) Which food is the least popular?

b) How many people like chocolate?

c) Which food is the most popular?

d) How many people like apples?

e) How many people altogether were asked what their favourite food is in this survey?

Amman created a chart to show the colour of cars in the school car park.

Black	Red	Blue	White	Green
✓	✓	✓	✓	✓
✓	✓	✓	✓	✓
✓	✓	✓		✓
✓		✓		✓
✓		✓		
✓		✓		

a) Put this data into the table with tally marks and show the totals.

Colour	Tallies	Total
Black		
Red		
Blue		
White		
Green		

b) On the day Finlay surveyed the cars in the school car park:

- 3 members of staff cycled to school
- 4 members of staff walked to school or got a lift
- 2 members of staff travelled to school by bus.

How many members of staff were in school altogether on that day?

14.2 Bar graphs

1 Use the information in the box to complete the pictograph about the children in Nuria's class.

Use this symbol to represent one person:

| Five people have green eyes. | Ten people have blue eyes. |
| Eight people have brown eyes. | Two people have hazel eyes. |

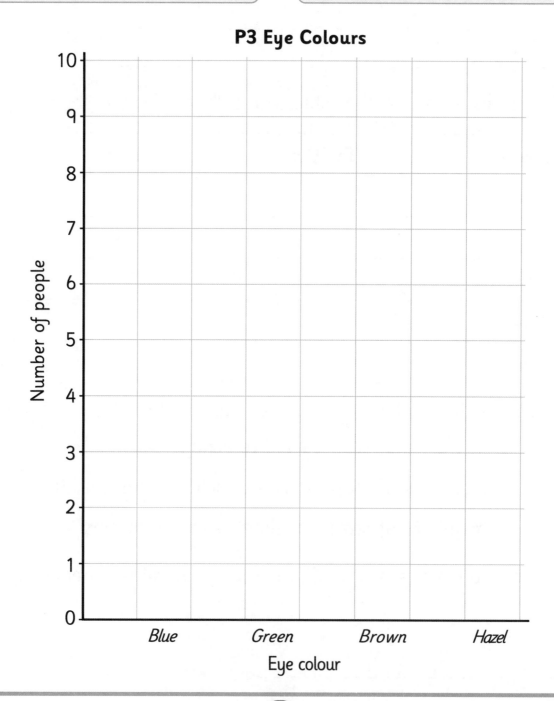

P3 Eye Colours

Number of people

10
9
8
7
6
5
4
3
2
1
0

Blue   Green   Brown   Hazel

Eye colour

2 Amman carried out a survey in his class. Fill in the totals to complete his tally chart.

Favourite Toy	Tally	Total
Football	卌 卌 |||	
Jigsaw	|||	
Dolls	卌 |||	
Computer	卌 卌 卌		

b) Use Amman's information to complete this bar graph.

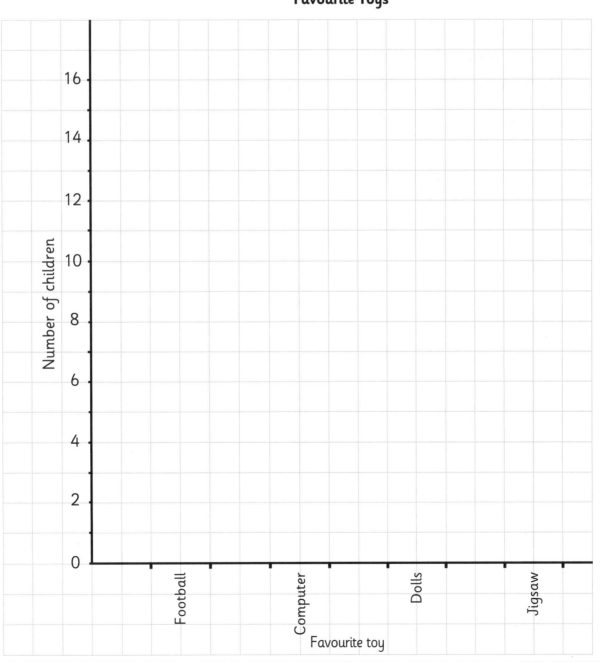

Favourite Toys

a) Complete the table by making tally marks for each total.

Favourite Fruit		
	Tally	**Total**
Apple		10
Orange		9
Grapes		3
Banana		5

b) Use the information in the table to draw your own bar graph. Remember to include a title and labels on your graph.

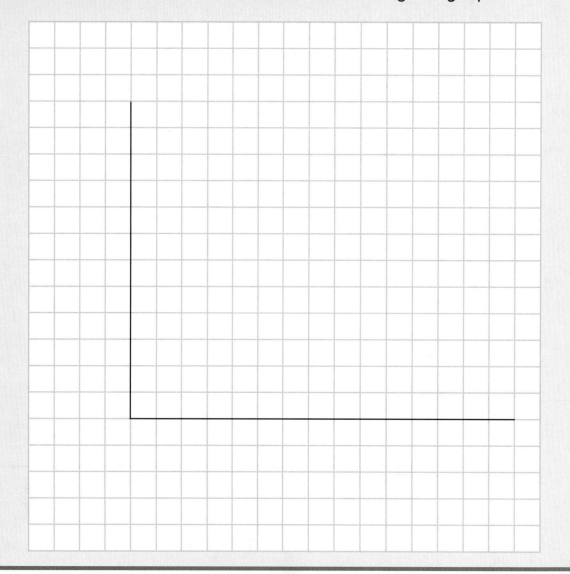

1 Nuria asked the children in her class 'What is your favourite shape?".
The bar graph below shows the results of her survey.

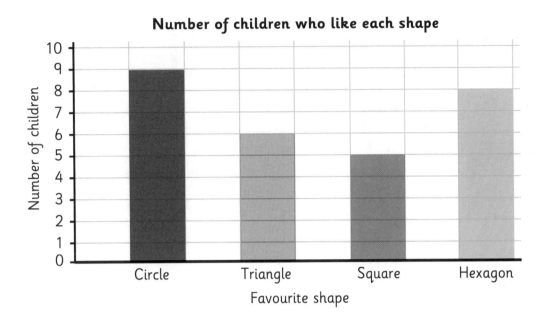

Number of children who like each shape

a) Which shape is more popular than
the hexagon?

b) How many more votes did the circle
get than the triangle?

c) Which shape was the second most
popular?

d) Which two shapes was the
hexagon more popular than?

e) The triangle was more popular than

the _____ but less popular than

the _____ .

2 Which of these two graphs does each statement refer to?
Tick the correct box in the table below.

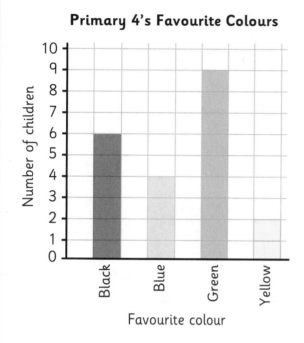

Primary 4's Favourite Colours

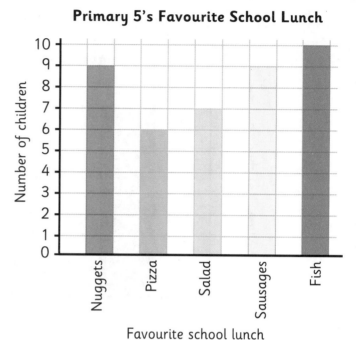

Primary 5's Favourite School Lunch

Statement	Colour	Lunch
The highest scoring category got 10 votes.		
The lowest scoring category got 2 votes.		
There were 41 votes in total.		
One category received 4 votes.		
One category received 9 votes.		